RUMOURS ᴀɴᴅ ODDITIES
FROM NORTH WALES

by
MEIRION HUGHES & WAYNE EVANS

A Selection of Folklore
Myths & Ghost Stories

GWASG Carreg Gwalch

First Edition: March 1986
Second Edition: May 1995

Text © Meirion Hughes/Wayne Evans

ISBN: 0-86381-337-2

Published by Gwasg Carreg Gwalch,
Iard yr Orsaf, Llanrwst, Gwynedd, Wales.

☎ *01492 642031*

Printed and published in Wales

Cover and Map Illustrations by David Rimmer

This book is dedicated to
Louise, David, Ruth, Jenny, Barry & Dylan

CONTENTS

Authors' Message to Readers

Many of the ancient tales, and theories regarding the murkier side of history, have their parallels in modern day life. If you would like to discuss any particular facet of Rumours and Oddities from North Wales, or share your views and friendship with the authors, your telephone call will be most welcome. Contact Meirion Hughes on Aberconwy (01492) 585109.

Meirion Hughes & Wayne Evans

Introduction

Celtic folklore traces complicated paths through historic and pre-historic times. In a book of this length, whilst limited to coverage of north Wales, it is impossible to deal with all the stories available. A thorough examination of fairies, alone, would require a thick volume of small print.

The authors have therefore attempted to present a variety of tales, including some ghost stories and even the odd historical theory or two, that will most entertain the reader. Where more than one version of an event exists the authors have merely chosen their own particular favourite.

Some of the views expressed in this book are not necessarily those of the authors.

Similarities to persons living or dead are purely coincidental.

Fairies, good or bad?

Of all its subjects North Wales folklore is particularly rich in fairy tales. Shrouded by time, myth and superstition, this magical race has always been the topic of fascination for both adults and children.

Welsh fairies are generally known as *Y Tylwyth Teg* (The Fair Family) and appear in a variety of sizes. Some are minute enough to hide in the folds of rose-petals. Some are as large as children. Others grow to the size of mortal beings.

The origins of the *Tylwyth Teg* are not clear. There are many theories but, according to an Anglesey legend, a woman living in the Holy Land, during the time of Jesus Christ, was terribly ashamed of the fact that she had twenty children. When, one day, Christ Himself approached her house, she decided to halve her shame by concealing ten of her children from Him. Those that were hidden disappeared. It is said they became the ancestors of the *Tylwyth Teg*.

Wherever they originated, most accounts hold that fairies established a kingdom underground and were in the habit of visiting our world through the medium of water. Lakes, riverpools, and submerged caves are all thought to be gateways to and from their land.

During frequent visits to our world, fairies loved to dance on moonlit nights and misty days. They often formed vigorous dancing circles. And because their young womenfolk were so captivatingly beautiful, mortal young men were often enticed to enter the dancing.

Once in the circle such men would be trapped, unable to stop dancing or break away from the circle for exactly one year and one day. The victim of this spell could only be rescued by someone outside the circle offering a branch of Mountain Ash — repellent to the fairies — with which to haul him out.

It was often difficult to convince men retrieved in this manner that they had been dancing for such a long time. To them it seemed a matter of only a few minutes. They were rarely tired, were not hungry or thirsty, and worn-out footwear was usually the only physical evidence of what had really happened.

Fairies, therefore, were a race that did not shirk from mischief and — according to some legends — evil. However, the majority of accounts attribute fairies with a great though sometimes puzzling wisdom, and also a certain degree of compassion.

So even if some were cunning and dishonest, most were well-meaning souls who appear to have enjoyed a mainly good relationship with humanity. Some fairies are even reported to have married mortal husbands — though it must be said that unions of this type rarely had a happy ending.

The Llanfrothen Legend

One such story concerns a young farmer who fell desperately in love with a voluptuous fairy girl who was in the habit of visiting the fields where he worked. For his part, the farmer was in the habit of begging her to marry him.

To begin with she declined, but continued visiting the farmer's fields. The more she declined, the more the young man persisted, and eventually the fairy — who must have had good reason for visting him — agreed.

But she did so conditionally, as do all fairies who agree to marry mortals. She said she would quite happily marry him and bring his children into the world. But if he ever struck her with any form of object made of iron, she would immediately return to the Fair Kingdom and he would never set eyes upon her again.

Of course the young man accepted this condition, confident he would never strike her with anything, let alone iron.

They married, lived happily, and eventually produced several healthy children.

Then one day as they were out riding together, the farmer's horse began to act strangely, kicking and bucking as though it had suddenly become wild. He warned his wife to keep her distance, but ignoring this she kept her mount pressed close to her husband's. Trying to regain control, the young farmer jerked his reins and the horse's head swung sideways, striking the fairy with the rein-bit, which unfortunately was made of iron.

Immediately the fairy wife told her husband she was leaving him for ever. He begged her not to go, pleading that it had been an accident, but she stubbornly ignored him. Greatly distressed, as he loved her so much, he begged her yet again. 'For the sake of the children!' he implored.

But still the fairy insisted she was leaving.

'What will become of the children without you?' cried the farmer.

'Let them be red-headed and long-nosed!' she screamed, and with that disappeared.

Neither the farmer nor his children ever saw her again.

St Collen & The Demon King

The town of Llangollen, Clwyd, site of the world famous International Eisteddfod, held there annually, is also the scene for a tale about an evil fairy king.

Llangollen derives its name from a 6th Century monk called Collen. The name Llangollen translates to 'Saint Collen's Church', in English. He was an ex-soldier who is said to have fought bravely against Julian the Apostate.

One day, whilst on his local travels, Collen encountered two men who were sitting on the side of the road, deep in conversation. As he approached he heard one of them mention a certain Gwyn ap Nudd, describing him as King of the Fairies and Lord of the Netherworld.

Angrily Collen turned on the pair and warned them not to speak of Gwyn ap Nudd as he and his followers were actually demons, followers of evil.

The two men, fearing the wrath of this charismatic figure, rapidly changed their topic of conversation to something less harmful. Collen observed them for some time before proceeding to his home on a hillside nearby.

That night as he lay asleep there came a loud knock at the monk's door. A crafty voice advised that this was a messenger from Gwyn

St Collen's Church

ap Nudd who was inviting Collen to visit the Royal Castle. Collen ignored the voice and returned to his sleep.

The same thing happened on the following evening. Again the request was ignored. Then finally on the third night a stark message was accompanied by a threat that if Collen did not accept the Fairy King's invitation, dire consequences would soon follow.

This time Collen deliberated for a moment, then politely informed the messenger that he would heed the invitation, but would it be acceptable if he paid his visit the next day? The messenger snorted his approval and left.

Collen arose the following morning, dressed and concealed a bottle of holy-water on his person. Before long the messenger returned and guided the unwilling guest on a tortuous route over hills and through marshes and forests. Eventually they arrived at a magnificent castle standing in the centre of a mist shrouded meadow.

Upon entering, Collen saw crowds of handsome young men and beautiful, full-breasted women who were all too obviously members of Gwyn ap Nudd's heathen court. They whispered and giggled as the monk crossed the great hall. But Collen ignored them, his features were like stone and his heart beat coldly as though chilled mercury ran through his veins.

The Demon King appeared. 'Welcome my dear friend,' he said. 'Welcome to the palace of the beautiful people.'

Disciplining himself against the Demon's charms, Collen declined to answer, and instead stared directly into the eyes of the Fairy King.

Apparently flustered by this resistance, Gwyn ap Nudd ushered the Monk into a banqueting room. They were followed by the preening members of the court.

Tables here had been laid with a banquet of dead forest leaves and decaying swamp rushes. Tankards were filled with the fermented sap of rotten oak trees. Wineglasses held green pond-slime which wriggled with tiny living creatures.

'Eat and be merry,' said the Fairy King. But, shivering, Collen declined, pointing out that this was the food of the dead. Death and damnation would come to any mortals who allowed such fare to pass their lips. The monk glowered at the sinful beings who were all too eager to feast on the tainted food.

Gwyn ap Nudd tried to engage Collen in conversation, using hypnotic words and phrases in an attempt to spellbind his guest. He drew attention to his followers. 'Are they not beautiful?' he demanded in a singing voice. 'Do you not think their robes are the height of good taste?'

Angrily Collen pointed that he was fully aware of the significance of the robes, which were blue down one vertical side and red the other.

'The blue,' he hissed, 'represents the freezing smile of the Devil. And the red, the burning fires of Hell itself.'

The Demon King turned swiftly. 'I will not suffer your insolence any longer!' he screamed, drawing a long, pointed sword. 'Now you will die by this blade, and in so doing will join the ranks of my faithful servants for eternity.'

The Demon lunged but Collen was well prepared. He swiftly

brought out his bottle of holy-water and threw its contents into Gwyn ap Nudd's face.

The Fairy King screamed, then with remarkable speed dissolved into a foul puddle on the floor. Collen's vision appeared to blur. The court of damned men and women shimmered before his eyes. Within seconds these bewitched souls, together with the castle and everything that had ever been involved with Gwyn ap Nudd, collapsed and faded into nothingness. Collen found himself standing in a bare meadow that was devoid of mist.

The evil fairy was never seen again and the Monk, when he returned to his village, was proclaimed a hero and a Saint.

Ancient Wells

Rejoining The Severed Head

Most famous wells in North Wales have some connection with a Saint. Perhaps the best known of these stands in the town of Holywell, Clwyd — the town being named after the Holy Well of St Winifred.

Said to possess healing powers, the waters of this well have been flowing since the 7th Century. In the 1880's the well, which is spring fed, was reported to be capable of discharging twenty tons of water a minute; it also fed an artificial lake and powered a watermill.

St Winifred is assumed in legend to have been instrumental in the formation of the spring which later developed into the present day spa — with all its claimed abilities to heal the sick and crippled. A beautiful young woman, she had chosen a religious vocation and vowed chastity in order to serve Christ.

However, a barbarous young man called Caradog, the son of a local chieftain, had other ideas about Winifred's chastity. Much to his disgust the girl had repeatedly rejected his advances. One day he was drunk on mead when he encountered Winifred on her way to evening worship.

Inflamed with lust he tried to tear the clothes from her body. But Winifred resisted vigorously; and so it was with a lewd and drunken anger that Caradog drew his sword and lopped off the girl's head.

Her guardian, St Beuno, who had been inside the nearby church at the time, saw what had happened and rushed to the scene. He cursed Caradog who died immediately. He then turned to Winifred's headless body. A new spring had emitted from the ground where it lay. St Beuno was not surprised: this was a gift from God; the girl had surely possessed purity of heart.

Confidently Beuno lifted the severed head and rejoined it to the torso. After a short prayer by her guardian Winifred recovered and only a thin line circling her throat indicated she had ever suffered such an experience.

Statue of St Winifred, Holywell

St Winifred's Well, Holywell

Beuno then thanked God and asked for all of Caradog's sinful family to be cursed to bark like dogs. Sure enough they were all afflicted in this manner and could only be cured if they bathed in the new well and sought penance from the Church.

St Winifred went on to become a nun and was made Abbess of Gwytherin, near the market town of Llanrwst. Her remains now rest in Shrewsbury Abbey.

In the shallows of St Winifred's Well today are stones which are strangely flecked with red. This is said to be the Saint's blood, spilled when she was beheaded thirteen-hundred years ago.

The Sting

St Beuno gained a reputation for rejoining severed heads and bringing people back to life. There are many accounts of him performing this miracle.

One example involved the daughter of Ynyr, King of Gwent. A handsome young rogue from Anglesey tricked the King into believing he was of high birth. For her part the Princess fell for the young man's good looks.

The King gave his blessing for them to be married and the pair set off for the rogue's 'palace' in Anglesey, loaded with gold and jewellery from the Gwent treasury.

The young man was greatly satisfied by his accomplishment. It was surely the biggest 'sting' he had ever performed in his life. The problem he now faced was getting away with it. He did not own even a home let alone a palace, and the Princess and the King would surely discover his treachery unless he did something brilliant.

He racked his mind for ideas. Schemes were woven one by one but dismissed by him as impossible.

Driven by desperation he camped for the night near Clynnog near the shoulder of the Llŷn Peninsula. The scoundrel kissed his besotted bride and ordered her to prepare for the night. When her back was turned, the youth drew his sword and lopped off her head. He then gathered the treasures and fled into hiding.

The story might have ended there if a passing shepherd had not discovered the roughly concealed body the following morning. The shepherd summoned St Beuno who happened to be staying at Clynnog at the time.

Beuno could see the woman was of noble birth and sensed she had been an innocent victim. He rejoined her head and the Princess revived, broken-hearted at the deceit to which she had been subjected, but alive again.

A well appeared in the ground where her body had spent the night. It became renowned for its powers to heal the blind and is known as *Ffynnon Beuno* (Beuno's Well).

Cursed and 'Un-Cursed'

It is said that during the 6th Century St Elian was travelling over the hills above the coast where Colwyn Bay stands today. He was very tired, very thirsty, but there were no settlements in sight. He had no choice then but to trust in God, and so sat on the ground and prayed for a warm night and some fresh water to quench his parched throat.

Even as he prayed, a spring emitted from the ground between his feet, and the saint drank gratefully.

In later years the well became famous for its powers. Unfortunately those powers were utilised mostly for negative purposes. The majority of people who used the well did so in order to issue curses against others who had offended or wronged them in some way.

In order to carry out such a curse, the 'client' approached the custodian of the well who would enter the victim's name in a register.

The custodian then performed a simple ceremony which involved carving the victim's initials on a pebble and placing it in the bottom of the well. Such services were not provided free of charge.

The majority of curses involved only minor ailments such as aches and pains, or bad luck. Death was rarely issued by this instrument.

Victims soon learned they had been cursed and in most cases visited the well in order to ask the custodian to remove it. This service was readily performed upon payment of a fee greater than that for the original curse.

The well was filled in during the 19th Century to discourage such practises.

Llangelynnin Old Church

Standing 927 feet above sea level and overlooking a picturesque part of the Conwy Valley, this secluded Church was built in the 7th Century by St Celynnin.

In the south-west corner of the walled churchyard is a tree shaded well. Many years ago the parents of sick children would come here to throw items of their children's clothing into the water.

If the clothes floated their child would live. If they sank, then the child was destined to die of its illness.

St Celynnin's Well

Mysterious Stones

Barclodiad y Gawres (The Giantess' Apronful)

The Roman Road between Ro Wen and Aber is a source of many stories. One of these is an account of two giants — husband and wife — who were travelling to Anglesey to build themselves a new house.

The husband was carrying two large stones, one under each arm, intended for the door-frame. His wife held a large quantity of small rocks in her apron.

As they walked along the pass now known as *Bwlch y Ddeufaen*(Pass of the Two Stones) they met a cobbler travelling in the opposite direction. The giants were not too sure of their route so naturally questioned the stranger, who pointed the correct way to get to Anglesey.

'And how far is it?' asked the giantess who had aching feet.

The cobbler, with a mischievous twinkle in his eye, glanced down at the dozen or so shoes he was carrying to be repaired.

Barclodiad y Gawres

Seriously he announced: 'I have worn out all these shoes walking from there!'

The giant moaned and dropped his two boulders. More dramatically the Giantess, utterly dismayed, threw up her arms in horror — thus emptying the contents of her apron to the ground.

This is why the rocks, which are still there to this day are called *Barclodiad y Gawres* (The Giantess' Apronful).

Carreg Lleidr (The Robber's Stone) Anglesey

In the 17th century, a market town was established at Llanerchymedd, Anglesey. This thrived and by the mid 1900's it boasted 250 boot makers. Llannerchymedd was nicknamed *Northampton Bach* (Little Northampton).

St Seiriol and St Cybi were in the habit of meeting outside the town. St Seiriol travelled from Penmon and always had the sun to his back — he became known as Seiriol the Fair. St Cybi from Holyhead, on the other hand, always travelled with the sun in his face and was known as Cybi the Dark.

In a field a few miles east of this spot is a stone shaped like a man carrying something on his back. A thief is said to have stolen a bible from a local church and because of the locality's Saintly connections was turned to stone as he fled.

According to the locals, every Christmas Eve on the stroke of midnight, the stone leaps from the ground and runs around the field three times.

Y Meini Hirion (The Tall Stones)

Not far east of Moelfre mountain, above Penmaenmawr, is a collection of stones wrongly known as The Druid's Circle. The circle may have been used by the Druids in later times but it was built roughly 1000 years before their appearance in this part of Wales.

During archaeological digs in the 1960's a cist covered with a capstone was discovered in the centre of the circle. Beneath were found the cremated remains of a child, estimated to have been

Carreg Lleidr, Llannerchymedd

about eleven years of age at the time of death. Close by, a smaller cist revealed more bones and also a small bronze knife.

There are two important stones in the circle: The Deiety Stone and The Stone of Sacrifice. It is claimed that if a person swears near the Deiety Stone, it will lean forward and strike him.

Opposite, the Stone of Sacrifice possesses a small hollow within its rock. Place a baby of less than a month old in this hollow and, according to superstition, that child will have good fortune for the rest of its life.

In later years it is said witches were in the habit of gathering at the circle and carrying out certain morbid rituals. At the height of one of these ceremonies the Stone of Sacrifice bellowed out a grim warning to the women. They fled in terror, except for two who had died of fright on the spot.

Maentwrog (St Twrog's Stone)

The village of Maentwrog is a few miles south of the slate town of
Blaenau Ffestiniog. In the churchyard, standing next to the porch,
is a stone of unknown origin.

According to legend, a giant called Twrog was disgusted by
pagan rites being held on the land where the church now stands.
After watching for a few moments from a nearby hill he threw a
large stone which hit the ungodly altar the pagans were using and
destroyed it. His thumb and finger mark can still be seen in the
rock.

Twrog himself settled in the area and his followers erected a
church where the boulder was embedded in the ground.

Maen y Bardd (The Poet's Stone) Burial Chamber

High above the village of Rowen in the Conwy valley stands the Maen y Bardd *Cromlech* (Burial Chamber). Locals call it *Cwt y Filiast* (The Greyhoundbitch's Kennel). A short distance away stands a tall singular stone of about seven to eight feet in height, which together with the cromlech is the subject of myth.

Many years ago a giant who was also a shepherd sent his dog out to bring back some stray sheep from below the long ridge of Tal y Fan. The dog proved to be disobedient and rested inside the burial chamber.

In a rage the giant threw his huge stick. It flew like a spear through the air until it struck the ground not far from the cromlech. This awoke the dog, who sensibly carried out his master's instructions from then on.

The stick turned to stone and is still there for all to see. It is sometimes referred to as Arthur's Spear.

Ancient Religions

The Druids of Anglesey

Druids were an order of Priests who organised themselves into a position of great power amongst the Celtic peoples. In the absence of institutionalised nationalism they became the ruling sect, and, according to the Romans, subjected ordinary people to brutal rituals in which mass human sacrifice predominated.

Druid activity in North Wales appears to have had its centre upon the Isle of Anglesey. Very little is known about their doctrines or history. Druids were very protective about their beliefs and the use of the written word was, apparently, forbidden in their religion.

Most documentary records available now have been left by the Romans, who invaded Britain in 54 B.C. Their legions descended upon Anglesey in 61 A.D.

Intent upon quelling this last bastion of Celtic resistance, they crossed the Menai Straits under the command of Suetonius Paulinus.

The Romans — on a rare occasion in their military experience — were temporarily disarrayed when they first saw the Druid forces.

Hardened soldiers were terrified by the remarkable sight of an advancing mass of heavily armed warriors which included wild women who brandished torches and shrieked like demons. White-robed Druids were all around, their sacrificial blades held to heaven, issuing dreadful incantations to the gods.

To the Romans, whose account this is, it appeared that terrible powers were being used by the Celts and the invaders suffered many casulaties during the initial phase of the battle. However, under urgent prompting from their generals, and with great discipline in the face of such adversity, the legions managed to reorganise and counter-attacked in classic formation. The Druids were quickly defeated.

In the years that followed, the Romans conducted a campaign to wipe out the Druid faith in this part of Wales. They were apparently sickened by Druidic rites which — according to the

Derwydda

Romans — included placing groups of people in wickerwork cages and burning them to death as a gift to the gods. But it is more probable that the Romans — who were not adverse to their own brand of ritualised cruelty — saw the Druids as a threat because of their ability to organise the population into a fighting force, and concocted stories similar to those of other Romans elsewhere in Celtic Europe.

Whatever the truth, the result was one of the very rare occasions Rome granted its authority to massacre a population.

According to some historians, the Druids continued a form of guerilla warfare against the Romans as the latter proceeded to destroy the sacred forests and tried to wipe out the people of Anglesey. There are blood-thirsty accounts of the white clad priests swinging down from trees with their curved knives and beheading Roman soldiers as they passed below.

Druids & the Wicca Religion

There is ample evidence that the Romans and later Christians failed to kill Druidic faith in North Wales or elsewhere in Europe. It can be argued that basic principles of the religion survive strongly to this day.

It is certain sacrifices to the Druid version of 'God' did occur but Roman motivation ensures their accounts, that such sacrifices were of humans, remain highly suspect. Indeed the pre-Christian Romans practised idolatry in their multitude of religions and slaughtered humans in amphitheatres in the name of simple entertainment. Druid sacrificial ceremonies were probably little more than symbolic gestures involving poultry or the burning of cereal.

Early Christian missionaries found they could only introduce their new religion if they were willing to compromise. Many Christian festivals and rituals have pagan tradition at their roots. Harvest thanksgiving is a prime example of a ritual dating back to Druidic times. Throwing coins into water, or wishing wells, is another.

Historians however have a great and sometimes pedantic

difficulty filtering what survives of Druidic faith from the confusion of cults, pagan doctrines and superstitious beliefs that have evolved through the ages.

Links between Druidism and witchcraft for example cannot be discussed seriously, as the term 'witchcraft' itself is one of total confusion and has more to do with the scattered folklore of peasant superstitions than with a specific religious belief.

What is certain however is that a religion known as Wicca has survived through history and continues to be practised in North Wales to this day. Indeed the concentration of so-called 'witches' living in North Wales today is probably the highest in Britain. The practitioners of this religion distance themselves from the mythological meanings of the word 'witch' and describe their faith as that of 'Wicca' or 'The Craft'.

The authors favour the theory that the original Druid faith was similar to that of other pagans scattered throughout the world. The North American Indian and Aboriginal peoples of the Southern Hemisphere possessed strikingly similar doctrines which compelled them to live in harmony with all living things. The belief that all things, including rocks, soil, water, air, were living things and carriers of the 'infinite intelligence' or 'force' was almost universal. That all living things deserved honour and respect was intrinsic.

The similarities between those ancient beliefs and that of the similarly ancient Wicca religion are compelling when distances of geography and time are taken into account.

One can only imagine the culture shock the Celts shared with the Indians and Aborigines when confronted by new races of people, who believed everything was dead, and who then proceeded with great energy to try to kill everything that was living.

There are other ancient sources which suggest that some of the old Greek philosophies and sciences were taught to the Greeks by the Druids. But nothing can be described as a certainty when discussion of the Druids takes place. By the same token only arrogance would suggest that nothing of their faiths, beliefs or science survives today.

One strong indicator, at least through the link of Wicca, can be found today in the strangest of places. It is the ancient belief that 'thoughts are things': that one needs only to think a thing strongly enough for it to become real.

Study of the many modern day books known as PMA's (Positive Mental Attitude) or self-improvement manuals, now widely used in all manner of business life, will reveal the powerful continuity of the 'thoughts are things' theory.

One need only picture something strongly enough to make it so.

Real Witchcraft in North Wales

The Penal Witchcraft Act, which was law from 1563 to 1736, made it an offence punishable by death for the causing of harm to a human being or domestic animal by the use of Black Magic. It was this act, generally duplicated in Scotland and Ireland, that led to the days of the Witchfinder General, the witch trials, and the putting to death of thousands of people, who by modern standards were innocent of any crime, and were, incidentally, in the vast majority, women.

A strange statistic looms up through history from those dark days. While Scotland, Ireland and England put to death thousands of so called witches. Wales struggled to sentence to death a total of four — and one of those managed to escape.

It is a confusing anomaly indeed when one considers that Wales with its roots as both the last bastion of Druidic resistance against the Romans and later the Celtic defiance of the Angles, Saxons and Normans, had the highest concentration of those actually practising the Wicca religion — the real witch-craft.

But it is easier to understand if consideration is given to the fact that Wicca, if generally understood and tolerated by a population, even though a rising majority practised Christianity, did not attract opinion that it was a religion of evil.

Witchcraft, as defined by Christian civilisation, was a destructive force, which used the powers of Satan to spread disharmony and evil throughout the world. Wicca, as defined by those who practised it, was the reverse. Those who lived alongside the religion in Wales during the days of the witchfinder, and who probably had an understanding of its principals may well then have been better equipped to tolerate it. Other factors which separated Wales from England were those of language and culture.

This attitude appears to be replicated in modern times in the United Kingdom. 'Satanic Abuse' scandals have been numerous in recent years. But they have not occurred in a North Wales which possesses a massive proportion of practising Witches.

The answer to why this is so might be found in a statement by a modern witch, living in Gwynedd, interviewed by the authors:

'Witches, real witches, do not believe in Satan, but believe only in the negative or positive forces which control our universe. Real witches use only positive forces, as they understand the fact that negative forces bring back the majority of harm upon the user.

'Christians believe in Satan as well as Christ. Satanists, in my opinion, can only be described as negative Christians.

'There are those, of course, in any race, creed, or religion, who are centred more upon negative than positive forces. They appear to be more in control of our world at present than the positive . . .'

The Stone Women of Moelfre

Many years ago there were three women in the village of Penmaenmawr whose daily task it was to separate chaff from grain. They did this by throwing wheat into the air so that the breeze blew away the light chaff and left the heavier grains to fall to the ground. The method is called winnowing.

That particular summer was the hottest anyone in the village could remember. For three days there had been no wind whatsoever. The smoke from cooking fires rose vertically and the women could not winnow the grain needed for turning into flour. Frustration set in and it was on a Sunday morning that one of the women suggested going to the top of Moelfre, above the village, where she was certain there would be a breeze.

Initially the others were dubious. It was Sunday and no God fearing man, woman or child worked on the Sabbath. But eventually they agreed to the idea and hurried home for sacks of grain.

They met in the village square. Each wore her working clothes:

One wore a red apron, another white, and the third a vivid blue. Stooping under heavy loads the trio worked their way up the steep path towards the mountain.

A farmer, who realised what they had in mind, shouted at them as they passed. He warned that God Almighty would damn them if they persisted with their sacrilege.

Ignoring him they continued and a little further encountered an old man sitting in the shade of a tree. Again they were warned but the unheeding women climbed on.

At last they arrived at the foot of Moelfre and began to ascend. A cold breeze could now be felt. It grew stronger as they climbed, until at long last when they arrived at the summit conditions were ideal for winnowing.

The woman in red set down her sack. Her friend in white opened hers, and the third in blue began the actual winnowing. But those were the last actions of the three women. In the blink of an eye they were turned to solid rock.

When searchers from Penmaenmawr reached the summit, they found three statues: one in red stone, the second in white, and the third blue.

Today there are no statues on the dome shaped summit of Moelfre, but there are three stones buried there. Only the tops are visible and unfortunately they are not coloured red, white and blue.

The Red White & Blue

Certain geographical locations have a habit of attracting events. Moelfre appears to be one such place and there is a rather strange and tragic footnote to the tale of the stone women.

The local yarn spinners of nearby Llanfairfechan say that on the morning of 7th January, 1944 an old farmer was searching the foothills of Moelfre for a number of sheep that had strayed from his winter pasture. It was a wet and miserable day. Low cloud obscured the mountain and the man was being pelted alternately by rain and hail.

He was climbing a low wall when he heard a deep rumbling

Memorial to the crashed Liberator Bomber

sound from behind him. It rapidly grew louder and the startled old man ducked to the ground. The noise was deafening; he was terrified, and to his dismay a huge shape passed overhead.

In the murky vapours he was unable to define its exact outline but he did see a stark pattern that was coloured red, white and blue.

Thinking this to be the demented spirits of the stone women, the old farmer retreated down the mountain to his home — where he locked himself in for the rest of the day.

The explanation is simple and tragic. In 1939 Britain had become enmeshed in the Second World War. By January 1944 an exhausted nation had been joined by its closest friend, The United States of America.

A Royal Air Force base at Valley, Anglesey, was an important buttress in an Atlantic bridge bringing men, weapons and aircraft into Britain.

Newly arrived was a B 24 J Liberator bomber together with its crew and cargo of aircraft spares. On the morning of 7th January the bomber, nicknamed 'Bachelor's Baby', took off from Valley en-route for a Strategic Air Command base in Watton, England.

The pilot, Lt 'Ace' Schultz, was not told of his destination; a B17 aircraft already in the air was to guide him. Unfortunately the weather was very poor. In low cloud, 'Bachelor's Baby' lost sight of her guide, and hopelessly lost, whilst boosting power in an attempt to catch up, the aircraft crashed on the slopes of Moelfre, where it burst into flames.

The farmer had seen its red, white and blue national markings during its final seconds of flight.

Six died as the result of the accident including the crew's mascot, a black and white terrier called 'Booster'. A small memorial now stands on the site, sharing the mountain with the Stone Women. Hill walkers who find pieces of wreckage place them by tradition at the foot of the slate plaque bearing the names of the dead.

Six others, including Lt Schultz, survived.

The Curse of Nant Gwrtheyrn

In the valley of Nant Gwrtheyrn stood a deserted village whose people, like the Stone Women of Moelfre, were cursed because of their disrespect for Christian beliefs.

The village of *Porth y Nant* (Port of the Steep Valley), after standing abandoned for many years has now been renovated for use as a centre for learning the Welsh language.

Overlooking the sea on the Llŷn Peninsula, this was once a thriving fishing community. Its people tended to keep themselves to themselves and were not fond of outside interference.

So the chief man, who was strictly pagan in his religious convictions, was not very impressed when three monks from the church of St Beuno approached the village. When they began lecturing about Christian Scriptures the Chief became even less impressed, angry is perhaps a better word, and so he ordered that the monks be driven from the village.

Supervising the operation himself, he and the villagers stoned the monks until they had retreated to a position of safety.

Reaching the head of the valley, the Holy Men looked back at Porth y Nant and issued religious damnation against the ungodly villagers. Each monk devised his own individual curse.

The first vowed that no man born in the village would again be buried on consecrated ground. Another said that marriage would not be possible between men and women born in the village. And the third cursed the entire place to become, eventually, a deserted shell, a ghost town.

From that day the community's years were numbered. The first part of the curse held true. All the men who died did so from drowning whilst fishing at sea, and their bodies were never recovered.

The young women of the village, fearful of the curse, always left the village to seek a husband from other valleys. Young men brought in their brides from other areas.

But some years later, when the village had at last converted to Christianity, two young lovers, both born there, decided to marry despite the curse.

On the wedding day it was customary for the bride to behave bashfully and conceal herself. It was the groom's duty to seek out her hiding place and carry her to the church.

The groom was confident. He had on his best clothes and had discussed the various hiding places available to his sweetheart. But when he tried to find her he failed. For an hour he searched but to no avail. The whole village, now fearing misfortune, turned out to help the young man.

They searched high and low, calling out the bride's name loudly. They went through all the houses and buildings, looked behind every tree in the surrounding woods and came eventually to the cliffs overlooking the sea. But there was no trace of the girl.

The groom was broken-hearted. His sweetheart had given him a small pup the previous day. He continued searching through the night, carrying the puppy in his arms.

At dawn the whole village turned out again. They searched every place twice, then a third time, until nightfall once more prevented them. Again the young man continued through the night, the pup still whining in his arms.

For the third day searching continued until at last the wise men of the village concluded that the girl had probably fallen from the cliffs and her body had been swept out to sea.

Sadly the villagers accepted this theory and so the search was called off — except for the young man who paced to and fro on the edge of the cliffs, pitifully calling out the name of his bride.

Nights passed, mornings dawned, and for days the villagers watched him growing thinner and thinner. He no longer shouted and his eyes stared out to sea as though he was blind to everything else.

Two villagers decided to try to reason with the young man. On approaching him they discovered the pup he was holding had died. Dragging the body from him they threw it into the sea — which proved too much from the demented young man who jumped after it. He was never seen again.

Some years later the village woodsman was felling a tree that had been struck by lightning. After some sawing he discovered it to be

The village of Porth y Nant, today a Welsh learners centre

hollow and inside, to his horror, he found a skeleton. It was a small person, the stature of a young girl. She had been wearing a wedding dress when she died and her skull sprouted long golden hair.

The poor girl had climbed the tree to hide in its branches. She had probably been giggling in happy anticipation of the day ahead. Then she had fallen into the hollow where her ankle became trapped. For days she had called out, pleading for the help which never came, until she eventually died of thirst and starvation.

Her remains were placed in a coffin and a funeral procession set off for St Beuno's Church. It never got there. On the way, the horse drawn cart lost a wheel and the coffin slid off, falling over a cliff onto rocks where it was smashed to matchwood. The bride's bones were washed out to sea.

Not long into the 20th Century, the third curse came true. The village became deserted. One by one, sick of the ill-luck which seemed to follow all who lived there, its occupants left, never to return.

Geological surveys have revealed that the ground in the valley is rich in iron and attracts a great many lightning strikes. It might, then, have appeared to the villagers that the Wrath of God was indeed against them.

The Legend and Ghost of Beddgelert

The Legend

In the 12th Century there lived a Prince of Wales known as Llywelyn ap Iorwerth. He was a man, fearless in battle and keen on the hunt, who owned many ferocious hunting dogs.

His favourite animal though was an intelligent hound called Gelert. The only dog allowed into the lodge, this was a domesticated creature who was as gentle as a lamb with the family.

He would accompany the Prince on his sometime solitary and contemplative walks. And was always faithful, even when the Prince was tired and irritable from worrying about his border wars.

One day Llywelyn and his wife went hunting, leaving Gelert to guard their baby son in the royal lodge.

It was a good day, deer were plentiful in the forests in those times, and the prospect of venison for supper delighted the party as it journeyed home.

However, the Prince's smile was wiped from his face when he entered the hunting lodge to check on his son. There stood the terrible sight of Gelert, panting heavily, covered from nose to tail in fresh blood. In the centre of the room the baby's crib lay overturned on the floor, yet more blood trickling from beneath it.

In a terrible rage Llywelyn drew his sword and, believing the dog to have killed his son, thrust the weapon deep into Gelert's throat.

Then as the stricken hound lay dying, the Prince heard an unexpected whimpering from the crib. Heart pounding he lifted it and discovered the baby lying on the floor, completely unharmed. Alongside the infant, slightly hidden under bloodsoaked linen was the body of a huge wolf, its throat ripped out.

Gelert, the lamb of the family, had defended his master's son in the manner of a lion.

Overcome with grief and remorse Llywelyn went to Gelert's side, but by now the brave animal was dead. Tears covered the Prince's cheeks. How bewildered his beloved hound must have felt to receive the sword instead of warm words of praise.

Gelert's grave

Llywelyn decided Gelert would never be forgotten. The hound, he decreed, was to receive the manner of burial normally reserved for noblemen, and two stones should be fixed to mark the grave.

To this day there are two stones to be seen in the village of Beddgelert (Gelert's Grave), and a simple memorial set between them describes the legend — the legend of Gelert and his Master Llywelyn ap Iorwerth, one time Prince of Wales.

The Ghost

Gelert's is a delightful story and few people can remain unmoved by its sadness. But many versions along the same theme appear all over the world. It is quite probable that the story of the faithful hound is a universal and early example of the ancient art of story-telling.

However, legend seems to attract further legend . . .

Times were hard in the 18th Century, and as well as vital agriculture, crafts, game and fishing, a community's survival depended on passing trade.

Beddgelert was no exception and it is believed that in the late

1700's a group of villagers conspired to create their own local legend, borrowing the popular yarn of the faithful hound, and adapting it to suit the history of the area.

They derived the name Gelert from Kelert, a 5th Century Celtic monk who may have lived and died at a long since vanished monastery in the vicinity of the village.

The ring-leader of the plot was a certain David Pritchard, landlord of the Goat Inn. His motive — to attract the tourists of the day, pilgrims and the like — was, unfortunately, one of simple profit.

But whatever the rights or wrongs, with hungry mouths to feed, and barefoot, ill-clothed children, the result of the contrived legend was that the village began to prosper. People travelled miles to view the grave; David Pritchard made his fortune as an innkeeper; and Beddgelert had been a thriving tourist attraction ever since.

For all his wealth, in 1821 David Pritchard died of a heart attack aged 52. It was a death too sudden to allow him time to draw up a will.

Perhaps it was a destined irony, or a joke by Llywelyn's insulted spirit, but after his death the shrewd landlord became a legend in his own right.

A strange tale survives him.

Some weeks after the burial, the Goat Inn was the scene of some fairly peculiar goings on. Footsteps were heard on the stairs during the hours of darkness. Strange noises were heard in bedrooms. And in one bar room in particular, the sounds of the fire being raked and irons rattled — a habit of the late landlord's — was an especially sinister occurrence.

Nothing was seen and no explanation could be found, even though some of the braver servants sat up watching all night.

It was decided that ignoring the phenomenon was probably the best cure and the household prayed for the disturbances to cease.

But instead of dying away, the odd events grew curiouser. Servants reported seeing David Pritchard himself, wandering around the village, dressed in his usual clothes. Others spoke of his ghostly apparition tapping at the door to the stables. And on one occasion he was spotted walking stridently along the pathway near Gelert's grave.

The village was in the grip of fear. People refused to venture out of their homes after darkness. Doors and windows were bolted tight and charms carried to bed.

There was one exception. An old farmer called Huw — once good friend and servant to the late David Pritchard — decided it might be a fine thing to see his former employer once again.

So even though he was quite frightened, he made it his habit to step out of the cottage after dark and occupy his time with simple tasks, without resorting to charms of any form. If David Pritchard needed a friend after death, then good old Huw was waiting.

Sure enough, after feeding a sickly calf one evening, the old man turned to see the ghost standing close by.

Huw shivered but was brave enough to call out his former employer's name. But, remaining silent, the spectre turned away, beckoning the farmer to follow.

Heart pounding furiously the old man followed his unearthly guide to the village graveyard. There, as if to ensure there was no mistake as to who this was, David Pritchard's ghost stood on its own grave.

The old man could see directly through the ghost. He could even read the inscription on the headstone.

With a trembling voice Huw questioned the Ghost. 'Master,' he said, 'your grave states that you lie at rest. Why then is your spirit so disturbed it haunts the whole village?'

The ghost answered sonorously. 'My dear Huw. There can be no rest for me until a certain task is carried out.'

The old man begged to be allowed to do whatever was necessary to fulfill this errand. The ghost sighed. 'I thank you old friend. At last I find a willing ear after weeks of fruitless search.'

Huw listened carefully to the instructions. He was to go to the inn the following morning and speak to the widow Pritchard. She in turn was to be instructed to lift the hearthstone in one of the bar rooms. There a pouch containing one-hundred gold guineas would be found. It was David Pritchard's hoarded legacy to his wife and children, and from it his old servant Huw was to be given two gold coins for his trouble.

Huw nodded that he understood and, with that, the ghost faded slowly away.

The next day the old man carried out his instructions. The coins were found and the old man received his reward.

The ghost has not been seen since, though the inn still stands in the village of Beddgelert. But perhaps if you visit Gelert's grave and then partake in the hospitality of the Royal Goat Hotel, you might hear David Pritchard's gentle laughter when you part with your money.

The Dragons of Dinas Emrys

Hard pressed by invading Saxons, the 5th Century British King, Vortigern, decided to build a fort not far from the village now known as Beddgelert.

He chose a dome shaped hill as a stronghold and set his engineers to work. But try as they might his masons could not establish firm foundations. Each stone laid sank deeper into the ground and the earth began to tremble and boil.

Trying to defeat this mysterious force, they made effort after effort, managing on one occasion to lay two courses of stone. But still the ground shook and the walls collapsed.

Vortigern demanded advice from his court soothsayers who were of the opinion that human sacrifice was necessary. To appease the hill, they said, a man who has no Earthly father must be slain, and his blood sprinkled on the trembling ground.

Perhaps because of jealousy they suggested Merlin who was living nearby. The magician had surely been fathered by a demon. Vortigern considered, he had to agree about Merlin's ancestry, and so the magician was summoned.

Merlin was understandably reluctant to have his blood sprinked in such a manner. So, using his powers of vision he suggested to the King that he dig deep beneath the foundations, where he would find the solution to his problems — and much more besides.

After much consideration Vortigern agreed, despite his soothsayers' vociferous urgings to have Merlin killed. Labourers were set to work and soon an underground pool was unearthed. When this was emptied, on Merlin's orders, two sleeping dragons were found. One was white, the other red.

The beasts awoke and began fighting each other. Spellbound, Vortigern and his followers watched. At first the white dragon held the upper hand and drove its opponent to the ground, scratching at it and tearing flesh from bone. But the red dragon kept fighting, even though it appeared to be finished. It clawed its tormentor in the manner of a cat, all four legs working away as it lay, pinned on its back. At last the white dragon retreated, snarling. The red in

Dinas Emrys

pursuit with flailing claws and gnashing teeth, until the pale beast eventually turned and fled.

Vortigern was much impressed when Merlin explained that the battle had been a prophecy which affected the King and the future of Wales. The magician explained that the white dragon had represented the Saxons and the red was a sacred symbol of Wales. It was an indication the Welsh would never surrender, even at their blackest moment, and would one day fight back and drive the Saxons from Britain.

This, it is said, is how the Red Dragon found its way onto the Welsh flag which is called *Y Ddraig Goch* (The Red Dragon).

Vortigern's fort was soon completed and no futher tremors were experienced. Merlin found favour with the King who named his fort Dinas Emrys in honour of the magician whose Welsh name was Myrddin Emrys.

In reality the Red Dragon was probably adopted from an English banner unfurled in honour of the victory at the battle of Cressy. A victory which had hinged on the tactics of Welsh archers.

Ghosts

The Golden Knight of Mold

For many years the people of Mold, Clwyd, had reported seeing a ghostly figure dressed in golden armour. The sightings seemed to occur in the area of a hill known locally as *Bryn yr Ellyllon* (Hill of the Goblins) which stands on the outskirts of Mold. People walking along a particular road were often confronted by the ghost. It usually gestured to those who saw it before walking off the road and disappearing into the hillside.

One frightened woman who saw the apparition went straight to the home of a local rector and swore out a statement.

Several years later in 1832 a local farmer, who wanted ballast to repair a road, instructed his labourers to remove some soil from the hill.

After working for several hours they unearthed a round stone that was not of local origin. The farmer ordered them to remove this, whereupon a rotting corpse was revealed. It was covered over with a golden corset.

After a short time the corpse disintegrated but the golden armour remains intact. It now resides in the British Museum and is made of copper with only a thin layer of gold on its outer surface.

What the men had uncovered was the capstone of a prehistoric tomb or *cromlech*. The armour, which dates back to the Roman occupation of Britain, is richly decorated with small circles of hammered gold riveted to strips of bronze, stitched to the piece with cloth. Amber beads decorate the edges.

There is no identification of the ancient chieftain, but some local historians favour Catigern, son of Vortigern.

The Haunting of Plas Mawr

This is a story of tragedy, medical incompetence, and grief driven desire for vengeance. *Plas Mawr* (Large Mansion), the site of the story, stands a few yards down the High Street from Lancaster Square in the centre of Conwy, Gwynedd.

The Elizabethan town house was built by a certain Robert Wynne between 1577 and 1580. The building has an unusual feature: it boasts exactly 365 windows, and its watchtower 52 steps — the number of days and weeks in the year. Steeped in history, *Plas Mawr* is considered an architectural masterpiece and is famed for its highly decorative mouldings in plaster.

But the house is more popularly famous for being haunted. An apparition has been seen in the Lantern Room and strange noises are heard in and around the house, especially during winter months.

So popular is the place with locals who have an interest in ghosts that some of them have remained in the haunted house overnight — usually doing this under sponsorship for charity. Most report seeing nothing. Others are reluctant to speak of their experiences. A few talk about the gloomy atmosphere which pervades the old building.

To get to the root of this haunting we must travel back to a cold winter's night in the 16th Century. The master of the house, Sir Robert Wynne, was expected home after a long absence fighting in the wars. His pregnant wife and three year old son were eagerly looking forward to his return, and for the latter part of the day had kept vigil from the top of the watchtower.

The hours passed, it grew dark, and still there was no sign of Sir Robert. Disappointed though she was, Lady Wynne decided it was far to cold to remain in the tower and so led her little boy slowly down the steps.

It was here that tragedy struck. Missing her footing in the gloom, the heavily pregnant woman fell headlong, dragging her son with her, so that they both tumbled heavily to the foot of the stairs.

On hearing this commotion, a maidservant rushed to the scene to find her mistress and the young boy lying injured. She acted quickly; with the help of other servants she moved the pair to the Lantern Room then sent word to summon the local Doctor.

There was a knock at the door a few minutes later. But instead of the usual Physician, a young stranger had arrived. He explained that the family Doctor was away attending to another patient and would not be available for at least an hour, perhaps longer. In the meantime, the young man explained, he was Doctor Dick and would do what he could until his senior arrived.

He was immediately taken to the Lantern Room and there, by lamplight, he made his initial examination. To the servants dismay the young Doctor grew very troubled. He explained that both the woman and child were in a very poor condition and beyond his own limited abilities. He suggested that another messenger be sent to find the more experienced practitioner and urge him to come to Plas Mawr immediately.

The servants complied but collectively refused to allow Doctor Dick to leave. Insisting that he do something for the injured pair, they locked him in the Lantern Room.

The servants waited outside, praying for the arrival of the older Doctor. They waited . . . and waited . . . Many hours passed and a feeling of dread certainty settled on the household. Then suddenly there was a furious hammering at the main entrance. The maidservant opened the door breathlessly. But there instead of the Physician stood Sir Robert himself, home from the wars at last.

On hearing the panic laden story he pushed the moaning servants aside and burst into the Lantern Room — to be confronted by the terrible sight of his wife, son, and premature baby, all lying dead on the floor.

Mad with grief and rage he scoured the shadows for Doctor Dick. But the young man had disappeared.

Amid much weeping and howling from them the stricken knight ushered his servants out, and vowing that he would not leave the room until he found the scoundrel Doctor, he locked himself in.

For the rest of the night he was heard issuing curses and oaths and demands that the Doctor reveal himself. Outside, the servants listened, shivering with misery and jumping from fright at the loud outbursts from within the room.

Finally at daybreak silence had descended. Some of the servants gathered at the door and, using a second key, slowly opened it to see what had become of their master. There on the floor, next to his

Plas Mawr, Conwy

family lay Sir Robert Wynne where he had taken his own life by plunging a dagger into his throat.

Doctor Dick was never seen again. It is said the terrified young man tried to escape by climbing up the chimney. There he may have accidently discovered one of the many passages and hiding places in the walls of Plas Mawr. Lost in darkness he may have suffocated by inhaling smoke from the hearth fires that would have been burning during winter.

And what of the messenger who was sent for the older Doctor? It appears he turned up many years later, an old man by that time. He explained that on his way to summon the Physician, he had been unfortunate enough to be press-ganged by sailors and until now had been sailing the seven seas. He was most upset when told of the young family's demise.

As for Plas Mawr, strange occurrences have been reported from time to time ever since. Doctor Dick's bones, blackened with soot, are said to remain somewhere in the house. Robert Wynne's ghost, still seeking vengeance, haunts the Lantern Room.

Perhaps as a mark of respect, The Royal Cambrian Society — who have had their headquarters at Plas Mawr since 1881 — have been in the habit of running annual Halloween dances, but this practise has ceased in recent years.

The whole story sounds very mysterious and supernatural. But there is a well respected theory regarding the legend. It is thought that later residents of Plas Mawr invented the story to prevent servants going to the Lantern Room — where the family were hiding a religious or political fugitive.

The Ghostly Squire of Pentrefoelas

One evening some workmen were returning home near the village of Pentrefoelas, and were passing an orchard which had belonged to the late Squire Griffiths. Agreeing that the long dead landlord had no further use for his apples, they decided to gather a few for their children.

The men scaled the high wall and dropped down into the

orchard, landing in tall grass and undergrowth that was littered with fallen fruit. All conversation ceased. The place was deathly silent and a strange mist drifted between the twisted trees.

Almost reluctantly the workmen started collecting apples. But they had gathered no more than three apiece when a bellow of rage assailed their ears. Turning, they saw a cadaverous figure, dressed in old fashioned clothes, staggering towards them and passing like the mist through the undergrowth.

All apples were dropped; the wall was scaled in panic, and the men fled towards the village, workboots clattering on the road as the grey dusk darkened quickly around them.

They slowed as they neared the village and paused to regain breath. Then suddenly a figure loomed from the shadows and growled in a voice that ripped the air.

The men scattered across the fields. They ran with the strength of the mortally frightened towards their houses. And they did not stop until cottage doors were bolted securely behind them.

Never again did they go near the Ghostly Squire's orchard.

The Mermaid's Curse

Stand on Telford's suspension bridge at Conwy, look down into the river, and you will have some idea of just how treacherous its waters are. Whirlpools twist and churn, the water boils, and there is a depth of darkness that invited nothing but a swift and inescapable drowning.

It is a river of many moods. Go to the quay on a sunny day and all the esturial glory will emerge: the dominant castle, the fishing boats; the smell of the sea, perhaps tinged with gentle fish odours.

Or perhaps you will hear the sound of a mocking female laughter and the smell from the river is the smell of death. Conwy, after all, is a town under a curse.

It is said that during an ageless time long ago, perhaps before the building of the castle, perhaps later, a group of fishermen were casting their nets in the estuary when they saw a remarkable sight. There, bobbing on the waves was a delightful creature with beautiful features and long black hair. Even more remarkable was the fact that instead of legs, she possessed a long, fishlike tail which flapped lazily in the water.

Initially the fishermen were very nervous. They had heard strange accounts about these creatures and great danger was associated with their sighting. Hastily the boats were turned about in order to avoid her.

Unfortunately, as though in fun, the mermaid pursued one of the boats, only to become entangled in its nets. Now the fishermen saw the look of fear in her face and decided there was no danger after all. They hauled her into the boat and took her ashore at Conwy.

Many people came to see her as she begged and begged to be returned to the sea. But now the fishermen felt powerful. They desired revenge. Many friends had been lost at sea and here at last was something tangible to blame. The fishermen vowed that the mermaid was never again to be set loose to wreak havoc and drown innocent men.

For the poor creature this was a death sentence. Just as men will drown in water, she suffocated slowly in the air.

But even as she died she cursed the men of Conwy. She cursed their wives and children, and their children's children. She cursed the town and its buildings; its future buildings. And vowed that forever there would be many drownings in the river and diseases, wars and disasters in the town, until such time the world had ended.

The curse sounded pretty powerful. No one knows what became of the fishermen responsible. And superficially it must be said that Conwy does not appear to have attracted more than its natural share of disaster.

The only notable tragedy outside of war happened in 1806 when the ferry from the East bank of the river capsized on Christmas Day, drowning all but two of its fifteen passengers. Of course the mermaid's curse was blamed.

A more recent oddity is connected with the site where the mermaid is supposed to have died. It was there that the old town hall was built. When it burned down in May 1966, a few locals said they had heard the mermaid's ghostly laughter. The land was developed as a library and civic centre but within two months of completion had burned down again. The mermaid's laughter was heard once more.

Construction work was undertaken for a third time and now, 'touch wood', the building stands apparently unaffected by the curse.

Sunken Cities

Llys Helig

The coastline of Wales has altered a great deal over the centuries and it is certain that a number of towns and villages disappeared under the encroaching tides.

Not far from where the mermaid met her end, out in Conwy Bay, is the supposed sunken ruin of a town called Llys Helig. This, if it ever existed, was built by Helig ap Glanmog in the 6th Century.

The fate of the settlement was foretold years prior to the disaster — its destiny a retribution for the sins of Helig's forefathers.

Perhaps if the man had been any better than his ancestors the prophecy might not have been vented. As it was, Helig was a regular butcher of the innocent, and frequented drunken orgies whenever he could. The town became a sort of Welsh Sodom, renowned by the decadent rich and despised by the innocent peasants who were sometimes put to death in the name of entertainment.

One day, as Helig was beginning a particularly crude orgy, the sea rushed in, inundating the town within minutes and drowning the sinners like rats.

The only survivors were innocents who scrambled ashore not far from the present day town of Penmaenmawr.

Llyn Tegid (Lake Bala)

Inundations were not restricted to the sea. Many lakes have submerged villages at their bottoms and years ago there was a town in the basin of the valley where *Llyn Tegid* now lies.

The community was ruled harshly by one of the cruellest men to have ever lived in Wales. When his wife gave birth to their first child he ordered a celebration to mark the event and a huge party was held in the palace.

A local harpist was summoned to play at the feast. The young man hated the ruler, but knew it would be unwise, and probably fatal, to refuse.

- Amwch
- Llannerchymedd
- HOLYhead
- Llangefni
- PenhÉsgyn
- Bangor
- B
- Caernarfon
- Snowd
- Be
- Nant Gwrtheyrn
- Nefyn
- Pwllheli

Llandudno

Colwyn Bay

Rhyl

Conwy

Holywell

aenmawr
eyre

RO Wen

Denbigh

mold

Llanrwst

apel Curig

Betws-y-coed

pentrefoelas

Penmachno

au Ffestiniog

estiniog

g

Corwen

Llangollen

Bala

Bala lake
(Llyn Tegid)

N

57

That night the musician played his heart out, but the drunken guests ignored him. Later as the party grew wilder, he heard a curious whispering behind him. When he turned he saw a small bluebird that was repeating one word over and over. 'Vengeance, vengeance,' it said whilst indicating for the harpist to follow it.

Unnoticed, the young man left the palace and followed the bird up a hillside. Then, still whispering 'Vengeance, vengeance,' the feathered creature flew away.

The harpist was now alone on the hill and was beginning to feel a little foolish for having followed a little bird onto a cold hilltop. He decided to try to sleep, so making himself as comfortable as he could, he lay down behind an oak tree and closed his eyes.

He awoke at dawn and looked down into the valley where the town should have been. Instead of the houses and smoke from early morning fires, instead of the palace of sin and iniquity, was a huge lake, and floating on the surface was the young musician's harp.

The little bird had saved the life of the only innocent blood in the town, and yet again water was the tool of retribution against an evil nobleman.

Lake Legends

Dark Water, Red Altar

Water, as we have seen, is the greatest ingredient of legend. *Llyn Dulyn* (Black Lake), overlooked by the imposing ridge of Craig Dulyn, is the sort of place much frequented by fairies, goblins and rainmakers.

It is said a causeway once ran into the lake. 17th Century people believed that anyone who visited this on certain festival dates: Midsummer's Eve, All Hallows Eve and May Day, would be able to see who of their community was about to die in the forthcoming year.

At the end of the causeway, now submerged, is a red coloured rock known as the Red Altar. It was believed that a person pouring water onto this would cause rain to fall the next day.

There are also strange tales of fish with bulbous eyes and deformed bodies. But there is no physical evidence to confirm such claims.

Llyn Dulyn

Llyn Morwynion (Lake of the Maidens)

In the days of banditry and lawlessness, the area of Dyffryn Ardudwy suffered a chronic shortage of women. It seemed that every child born was male, and as years passed a generation of maturing young men found themselves in a position where prospective brides were the subject of intense competition. Fierce duels were fought with many resultant deaths.

Three leisurely youths, who preferred drinking ale to fighting duels were nevertheless keen to procure attractive wives for themselves. Meeting in a local tavern their conversation invariably turned to the subject of the fair sex. Beer drinking gave vent to romantic tendencies, if not their competitive zeal, and talk centred on how they might do this or that to win fair brides. By the end of such an evening the bottom of an empty jug still gave no clue as to how they might accomplish their aims in reality.

One night, the soporific trio expanded their imaginations and discussed leaving the area to pursue their cause.

Rumour had reached them that the Vale of Clwyd was bursting with suitable young wenches and a decision was taken to set off the next day.

Morning dawned and the three left the village on horseback. They arrived at their destination in Clwyd after two days travel, setting up camp in a secluded part of the Vale.

For the next few days the youths stalked the area for attractive females. Whenever they found one on her own they pounced on her, tied and gagged the poor creature, before dragging her back to camp. It was not long before they had three wriggling captives.

The girls wept and wailed as the men tried desperately to comfort them. It was explained that no harm was intented. A good life was waiting and they would be well treated. But the women were oblivious to all entreaties.

Of course the young men were rather tongue-tied without a jar of ale and were naturally unaccustomed to girls. They tried to present an attractive picture of their village, giving accounts of the delightful flavour of local ale. But at this the women screamed even louder.

Eventually the lads bundled their captives onto horses and began their journey homewards. As the tension eased the girls began to talk. One intelligent voice gave an account of the 'boring and strict life' she had been leading. Another agreed similar experience, and the third gave the opinion she was glad they were being taken as brides. By nightfall the women had been untied and were journeying willingly with what they now realised were three charming bachelors.

They made camp on the banks of a mountain lake, and in the morning the girls prepared breakfast, already practising their roles as wives. Later they bathed together in the lake. But as they laughed and giggled, splashing about in the water, several riders appeared from the forest. Terror struck the party. The three youths ran for their weapons, but were too late. They were cut down, hacked to death with axes and swords.

The horrified girls then recognised the horsemen to be their fathers and brothers. Weeping, they ran back into the lake and deliberately drowned themselves.

The girls had chosen death in preference to life without their newly found loved ones. The lake is hence called *Llyn Morwynion* (Lake of the Maidens).

The Floating Island of *Llyn Dywarchen*

A strange account of a water legend is to be found near Beddgelert at *Llyn Dywarchen* (Lake of the Turf Sod). In his book *A Journey Through Wales*, published in 1188, Giraldus Cambrensis refers to the lake as possessing a small floating island.

This, Giraldus claims, floated back and forth across the surface of the lake. It was so secure cattle occasionally stepped onto the island, chewed grass for a while, then stepped off when it next came near to the bank.

The astronomer Halley, discoverer of the comet named after him, is said to have visited the lake during a tour of Wales in 1658. He swam out to the island to test the legend. Using a wooden paddle he was able to steer the island around the lake and confirmed that it did indeed float.

Llyn y Dywarchen

Today there is an island in *Llyn Dywarchen*, but it is far too large to be capable of floating.

Llyn Idwal (Idwal's Lake)

During the beginning of the 12th Century, a Prince of Gwynedd by the name of Owain, son of Gruffudd ap Cynan, was involved in a war against the forces of King Hywel of Powys.

Owain had many sons, but his favourite, the youngest whose name was Idwal, was a very talented young man. Not at all suited to the rigours of war, Idwal was nevertheless popular with everyone. And it was generally accepted that the youngster was destined to become a scholar rather than a warrior.

His father, the Prince, was extremely proud of this fact, but also realised that the young lad was something of a liability. He could not take him to war, but neither could he leave him at home — marauding infiltrators from Powys might seize the opportunity to kidnap his son and hold the whole of Gwynedd to ransom.

Owain had no intention of facing such a dilemma. He decided to send the boy to live with his cousin Nefydd who lived on the banks of a secluded lake.

Now Nefydd was an extremely handsome man, and unfortunately somewhat vain. He called himself *Nefydd Hardd* (Nefydd the Beautiful) but to his eternal dismay his only son, Dunawt, was completely the opposite. To rub salt into the wound Dunawt seemed incapable of following the teaching's of his father, who was a recognised academic specialising in the arts.

Young Idwal's imminent arrival was, at first, welcomed by Nefydd, who was hoping his son would compare favourably with the Prince's boy.

But jealousy set its insidious roots as soon as Nefydd saw him. Idwal shone like a bright jewel beside the rather dull and bumbling Dunawt. And as time passed matters worsened; during lessons it seemed that whatever Dunawt could do with mediocrity, Idwal would accomplish with excellence.

Nefydd's jealousy grew to insane proportions. One morning he suggested to Dunawt that he take Idwal for a walk around the lake, telling his son to head for a particularly deep part. There, Nefydd suggested, he was to push his cousin in. Dunawt laughed and agreed, but knew full well what his father had in mind. This was not a joke, Idwal was unable to swim and would surely drown in such deep waters.

The young Prince happily agreed to walk with his cousin. He believed Dunawt to be the best friend he ever had.

So the two boys set off together, Idwal singing merrily in the early morning sunshine. Upon reaching the point where the bank was steepest, Dunawt pushed roughly and Idwal fell headlong into the icy cold water. As he struggled, and spluttered and pleaded for help, he saw that Dunawt was laughing on the bank. Confused and hopelessly alone with his father miles away, Idwal at last let water enter his lungs, and drowned broken hearted.

Owain was informed of his son's death and soon arrived at his cousin's home. Many days of questioning followed. Nefydd cleverly parried the accusations. But his son was clumsy and too idiotic to be capable of concealing his guilt.

The Prince would have had them put to death, but in the absence of witnesses his conscience would not allow him that satisfaction. Instead he banished the family from his Kingdom and stripped them of all rank and title.

Nefydd, with all his vanity, would probably have preferred death.

Owain ap Gwynedd decreed that the lake be named after his son and to this day it is called *Llyn Idwal* (Idwal's Lake) — the place where a young boy was murdered by people he loved and trusted.

The Devil in North Wales

There are many strange superstitions concerning the Devil in North Wales. Indeed, until the mid-nineteenth century, some people continued to believe in his physical existence. Houses were protected from the Devil by whitewashing the front doorstep, a practise continued by a number of households to this day.

It was believed the Devil's messengers were such diverse creatures as dragon-flies. He was able to appear in many disguises: ravens, black dogs, black pigs, or a stone rolling down a hill. Sometimes his presence could only be felt by those he came close to; this manifested itself as irrational terror or pure panic. The following story is about one site where such unseen manifestations are said to occur.

The Devil's Tree

Along Llanrhos Road, near Llandudno, stands the remains of an old oak tree which is supposedly the Devil's very own.

In the mid 1800's the Curate of the Parish, Rev. W. Arthur Jones, reported that his horse always reared up when passing the tree. On hearing this, a servant decided that the Reverend should be accompanied on his next trip.

A few days later the clergyman decided to visit Glan Conwy and he and his servant set off on horseback. On approaching the tree both horses reacted violently and the two men were convinced that the animals could see something that was not visible to the human eye.

But the story was not widely reported until a few years later when a cobbler from Glan Conwy had a mortifying experience along the road.

Cadwalader Williams was in the habit of delivering repaired shoes and collecting payment on Saturdays. He usually finished off at Llanrhos where he would buy a few groceries, before partaking of a few jars of ale at the local pub.

One particular Saturday, this ageing character had drunk one too many, and during his walk home along Llanrhos Road, instead of taking the opposite side of the road as he usually did,

Cadwalader actually approached the Devil's Tree. His senses dulled by alcohol he began shouting abuse at it.

Suddenly something hot and hairy landed on his shoulders and gripped him tightly about the neck. Cadwalader gasped and struggled but could not dislodge the creature. With no other alternative he began to stagger along the road, desperately hoping that he would see someone to help him.

He saw nobody, but after a nightmarish walk managed to reach the village of Towyn where he struggled to the door of a friend's house.

Nearly asphyxiated from the grip at his throat, he was almost dead when the door was thrown open. Then to Cadwalader's blessed relief the weight was suddenly gone.

The friend did not see the monster — but he did see what looked like scorch marks on the old cobbler's throat.

Visit the tree today and you might find it does possess some dark atmospheric power to chill. One of the authors of this book interviewed a young woman who had cycled past the tree at night and was taken by such fear, for no apparent reason, that she jumped off her bicycle and ran as though her life depended on it.

She was not aware of the legend at the time and did not hear of the Devil's Tree until she was contacted in connection with research for this book.

Some locals also speak of the ghost of a headless coachman prowling along Llanrhos Road. He is supposed to have driven his coach along the road at a terrible speed and was decapitated by a low hanging limb from the Devil's Tree.

Three Card Brag

The family at Henafon Farm near Rhuddlan were enjoying the best party they had thrown for years. Wine flowed, the guests danced to the lilting tunes of the fiddler. Young men gazed into the eyes of the pretty girls, danced with them and then drank from the plentiful supply of ale at the house.

By about eleven o'clock the guests, many of them drunk, started leaving. Most of them were farmers and knew that a late night would not be taken into account by their herds at the crack of dawn the next day.

Three young men who had no such responsibilities in the morning decided to stay a little longer. The hosts were tired, so showed the trio into a back room where there was a roaring fire in the hearth, a barrel of beer in a corner and a pack of cards on the table. They were told to stay the night if they wished, but to keep the noise down.

The youngsters readily agreed and sat down to play cards. At first they played for fun, but soon one of them suggested they should make things more interesting. By now the ale was flowing steadily and the others were not adverse to a little flutter.

'Three card brag,' said one of them, and dealt the cards. At that moment a clock on the mantle-piece struck midnight, and what happened then was remembered by all of them as if it had been a strange and vivid dream.

The door to the dimly-lit back room creaked open and standing there was a man, about the same age as them, but dressed all in black.

'Ah there you are,' he said with a friendly smile. 'I was about to leave, but our hosts said I might find a game going on back here.'

'I didn't see you at the party?' questioned one of the youths.

'I had business in the parlour,' replied the stranger. 'Besides, dancing with girls is of little interest to me.'

The young men nodded. They hadn't had much luck either. They agreed to let him join in the game. Four players would be much better than three.

The man in black lifted the pack, cut the cards skilfully and shuffled. 'What game shall we play?'

They told him — three card brag.

The stranger's smile widened. 'How wonderful, my very own game!'

At first they played for pennies. The stranger won most of the hands. Next they played for shillings and the man in black kept winning. He smiled charmingly at the others as he raked in his winnings, sympathising with their bad luck, and ingratiating himself by carrying out the chore of pouring fresh ale into empty tankards.

Not more than two hours had passed before the stranger held all their money.

'Oh dear dear,' he said as he studied the pile of coins on his side of the table. 'This is most unfortunate. Do you know what? I would so dearly like you to have the chance to win this back,' he smirked, 'but you have no money left.'

The young trio agreed, they were indeed penniless.

The stranger cut the pack, shuffled the cards. 'But I do know a way,' he advised. 'We'll play for stakes higher than mere money.' He reached into the pocket of his black coat and pulled out a thick wad of banknotes, threw them onto the table.

'Wager to me your most valuable possession and I guarantee you will all win.'

The young men, eyes red from the ale, stared hungrily at the fortune now sitting on the table.

'With what can we wager?' asked one of them.

'Your most precious possession,' the stranger answered.

'What might that be?' asked the second.

'Your eternal friendship,' said the stranger.

'Seems a small price to pay,' said the third.

The man in black threw his head back and laughed heartily. One of the cards in his hand fell to the floor.

The nearest youth reached down to pick it up, his head dipping below the table, eyes searching for the lost item. He surfaced with the ace of spades in his hand and a look of total terror in his eyes.

'Devil!' he wheezed, his breathing laboured.

The stranger smiled. 'Cards?'

The two others, sensing trouble, ducked their heads under the table. There they saw that the strange man wore no shoes. And instead of feet he owned a pair of hairy, cloven hooves.

'Devil!' they both shouted.

And with that the man in black shimmered in the firelight, dissolved into a cloud of white smoke which then flew into the hearth and disappeared up the chimney with an air ripping bang.

The money on the table turned to dust.
The young men thanked God they had escaped with their souls.

The Magical Huw Llwyd

The Witches of Betws-y-coed

Just outside the village of Betws-y-coed, years ago, stood a Coaching Inn with a rapidly declining reputation amongst stage coach travellers. Passenegers on their way from London to Holyhead, who stayed there overnight, frequently complained of being robbed in the night — despite the fact their bedroom doors had been locked from the inside.

Officers of the law found it impossible to solve the problem. No evidence could be found; there was no obvious culprit; the door locks were not false, but still money kept disappearing. It was like magic.

Eventually a Professional Conjuror by the name of Huw Llwyd was called in. He accepted the assignment, provided he had his fee in advance, and provided that it was not necessary to deliver a culprit. The coaching companies were desperate and the terms were agreed.

Huw arrived at the Inn dressed as an officer in the Army, which he had once been. Concealing his true identity, he told the owners, two sisters, that he was on his way to Ireland via Holyhead.

That night during the evening meal, Huw entertained the two sisters with tales of his army life, and he made a point of saying that he was carrying a large amount of money, with which he intended securing property in Ireland.

Eventually he yawned and excused himself to go to his bed. But first he asked the sisters if they could provide him with additional candles. Because of his Army experiences, he explained, he could not sleep without candlelight.

Huw went to his room and locked the door behind him before lighting candles in each dark corner. Satisfied with the lighting, he undressed and climbed into bed, concealing his drawn sword under the bedclothes beside him.

Time passed, silence reigned, except for the occasional hoot from a passing owl outside the window. Huw closed his eyes but

70

did not sleep, remaining like that for hours, his senses alert and his breathing silent but steady.

Eventually he heard a faint noise within the room. The conjurer opened his eyes slightly and saw two small cats climbing down the partition wall dividing his bedroom from the next.

The cats crept around the room sniffing and searching. They then approached the chair next to the bed where Huw had hung his uniform. One of them slid a paw into the trouser pocket where the conjuror kept his purse.

Suddenly, Huw leapt up, sword in hand, and struck the offending cat's paw with a single flash of polished steel. There was a terrible scream and the animals shot across the room and disappeared.

The following morning, the Conjuror appeared for breakfast and immediately noticed that only one of the landladies was present. When asked, she explained that her sister was unwell and was resting in bed.

Huw smiled and ate his breakfast, but when it was time to leave he insisted on saying farewell to the sick woman. Her sister resisted at first but eventually agreed when she saw the uniformed man's hand move to his sword hilt.

He was taken to a room at the back of the Inn where the supposedly ill woman was seated in a chair, not in her bed. Huw offered a cheerful good morning, explained he was leaving, and offered his hand in farewell. The sick woman offered her left in return. But Huw refused, saying that he could not accept a lefthanded handshake. He patted his sword in grim emphasis.

The woman trembled and removed her right hand from beneath her shawl. It was wrapped in bloodstained bandages, and quite obviously three of her fingers had been crushed. At this Huw revealed his true identity. He told the pair he was fully aware of their witchcraft and that any further stealing of this nature would be met with dire consequences.

The two witches heeded the warning and counted themselves lucky. After all, Huw Llwyd was a magician, a fellow of sorts, and

Huw Llwyd's Pulpit

had they been caught by an ordinary person, they would surely
have hanged.

Professionals protected their own, even all those years ago.

Huw Llwyd's Pulpit

After dealing with the witches, Huw Llwyd returned to his home
outside Ffestiniog and resumed his normal lifestyle — that of a
conjuror. Sorting out the two sisters had been mere detective work.

There were many conjurors or wizards in North Wales during
the 17th Century. They generally claimed to be the seventh sons of
sevenths sons and usually found employment removing curses
from troubled people. The fact that curses were both issued and
removed by the same profession does not appear to have targeted
the ordinary population against this monopoly.

Some wizards, it is said, were men who sold their souls to the
Devil. Such a person would first have to deny Christ's Divinity; he
would do this by going to a Holy Well, where he would take a

mouthful of sacred water and spit it out in a derisive manner. The Devil was then certain to make contact.

But most of the profession derived their supposed powers from education and were labelled 'Wizards' by the simple people around them. Amidst a mostly illiterate population, a well-read man would have been thought magical.

Huw Llwyd was almost certainly highly intelligent and brilliantly educated, but because of his profession of Conjuror, where an income depended on fees from the superstitious, he had to maintain a certain image.

Not far from his home, standing in the centre of the River Cynfal, is an oddly shaped stone that was Huw Llwyd's pulpit. He was in the habit of standing on this to issue incantations to the powers of the Earth. This act usually drew an audience, from whom the magician demanded great respect.

However, on one occasion a local farmer who did not believe in such things had the affrontery to heckle and throw insults at the Demon Preacher.

In a terrible rage, Huw Llwyd cursed the farmer, using powerful and sinister words. A few days later, the unfortunate man's cattle began dying.

Eventually the farmer was forced to call at Huw Llwyd's house and beg forgiveness. The magician agreed, he had no wish to cause unnecessary suffering, the curse would be removed. Of course the farmer was obliged to pay the standard fee for the service.

Huw and the Ghost

With a steady income, the magician was able to afford the luxury of a family. He chose for himself a wife with a lively sense of humour. As well as bringing his daughters into the world, she was in the habit of playing tricks against the wizard.

One night she sent her brother down to the river where Huw was practising the nocturnal version of his act on the pulpit.

The magician's brother-in-law draped a white bedsheet over his head and crept up behind the preacher. Without looking back,

Huw stopped his normal incantations and spoke quietly but with massive underlying power.

'If thou art a good spirit, thou will do me no harm . . . If thou art an evil one, thou will do me no harm as I am wedded to a sister of thine. Now, thy white one, beware of the Black One behind thee!'

Huw's brother-in-law returned to the house, his face whiter than the sheet he had been wearing.

The Bandits of Pentrefoelas

One evening, whilst on his numerous travels, Huw Llwyd called at an inn at Pentrefoelas, near Betws-y-coed. Some accounts place this as occurring during his journey home after dealing with the witches. It must be said though that very little is written about the conjuror, and most of the stories are quite literally word of mouth folklore handed down from generation to generation.

Not long into his meal Huw was approached by three powerfully built men. They sat down uninvited at his table and proceeded to try to intimidate him.

One of them told Huw he would be lucky to leave the inn that night without having his throat cut. Another said his favoured method of killing was strangulation. And the third patted the haft of his sword as he explained how much he enjoyed studying the varied colours of intestines he spilled from his disembowelled victims.

Huw merely smiled and continued eating.

At first the three bandits were amazed. Then they grew angry.

'You will die this evening,' one of them promised.

'In great pain,' said the second.

'And without dignity,' added the third.

'You're probably right,' said Huw, and winked mischievously at the men.

'Who is this man?' one of the bandits demanded plaintively.

One of his companions slid Huw's supper away from him across the table and stared into the conjuror's eyes. 'You would be most foolish to defy us,' he hissed.

Huw smiled. 'Then count me as a fool.'

'Who is this man?' repeated the plaintiff bandit, louder this time.

At this, the landlord glanced across the room. 'I'm not sure,' he said. 'But I think he's that magician from near Ffestiniog.'

The bandits considered this for only a fraction of a second before the eldest asked: 'What is your name?'

'What is in a name?' Huw countered. 'What does a mere name matter unless it can be spoken in friendship?'

At this the eldest bandit drew a dagger and held its point against Huw's unflinching throat. 'I have had just about enough of your impudence,' the outlaw warned. 'Hand over your money now and we might allow you to live. Defy us further and you will die this minute.'

Huw's eyes widened slowly but he rapidly assessed the other people in the room. Nobody there seemed the least interested in what was going on at his table. Most of the men there were drunk, crooked or puny. Most of the women were types who would have been quicker to slit his throat than the bandits.

'Nobody here will lift a hand to help you,' the leading outlaw told Huw, smiling to reveal huge black gaps in his mouth.

'Great,' Huw said casually. 'Then I have no alternative but to pay you what you so obviously deserve.' The magician waved a hand over the table. Miraculously the air glinted and there materialised on its surface a cow's horn that appeared to be made of solid gold.

Huw retrieved his supper and, totally relaxed, finished eating as the bandits stared, mesmerized at the horn.

After dabbing his lips with a napkin, Huw rose and made to leave. He approached the landlord and pointed casually at the bandits who were still staring motionless at the golden item on the table.

'Don't try to move them' Huw warned. 'Or you will become like them. And don't try to lift the horn as it exists only in the minds of idiotic men.' And with that the magician left.

The three bandits were found staring at an empty table when officers of the law arrived the following morning to arrest them.

Returning the Books

Some years later when the wise man was lying on his death bed, he summoned one of his two daughters and instructed her to take his collection of books to a certain spot along the river. There she was to throw them into the water.

She agreed and carried the collection to a place known as *Llyn Pont Rhyd Ddu*, (Pool of the Black Ford Bridge). But the girl was an avid reader and was against wasting the books, which were very old and valuable. She decided to hide them nearby.

Upon his daughter's return, Huw asked what had happened when she threw the books into the water. She replied that nothing had happened. Angrily, the conjuror told her to return to the river and, this time, carry out his instructions to the letter.

Shamed, the girl walked to the river and obediently threw the books in. Just before they hit the water she saw two huge hands break the surface. These caught the falling volumes before drawing them into the depths of the river.

The shocked daughter ran home to tell her father what she had seen. At this, a relieved Huw Llwyd said: 'Now I can die in peace.' Which he promptly did.

Some Mythological Witches

The Llanddona Tribe

Whilst the majority of witches were haggard old women usually living on their own, it is said a whole tribe of them once landed on the shores of Anglesey, near Llanddona.

Horrified by the appearance of these strange women, and their menfolk, the locals tried to drive them away.

But their leader, a grotesque, fat old woman by the name of Bella Fawr, issued a curse that caused a spring to emit from the ground. The local inhabitants mistook this to be a Christian miracle and so allowed the strangers to remain.

It was not long though before the tribe caused misery and terror amongst the population.

The men earned a living by smuggling. Law officers attempted to stop the practise on many occasions, but always failed due to the fact the smugglers had one particular weapon that was very effective at keeping enemies at bay. Each of the tribe wore colourful neckerchiefs and upon the approach of any man who tried to oppose them, they would untie these to release an evil fly which attacked the eyes of their foes and temporarily blinded them.

The female witches for their part were in the habit of going from door to door in order to beg for food. Refusal would be met by a curse. It is said they never paid for items they took from the marketplace, such was the fear they struck into the hearts of the traders.

The Magic Hare

Many witches could turn into animals at will. One such creature lived in Llanfrothen with her grandson Ifan, who earned a living for them through casual labour.

When he reached his teenage years Ifan developed a reputation as a game-beater and his services were much in demand. No matter what the conditions, or the shortage of game, Ifan always managed to raise something for the gentry of the area to chase.

Over a period of time however the huntsmen noticed that very often Ifan would raise a very large hare which then ran so fast and was so crafty it could never be caught. They became convinced it was always the same creature and that it was bewitched in some way.

Seeking the advice of the local priest the huntsmen were told that the only way a magic hare could be caught was by the use of a black dog that had no white fur on its body whatsoever.

Such a dog was purchased and Ifan's services were secured the next day.

Sure enough Ifan very quickly raised the big hare and the huntsmen and their new dog set off after it. This time the hare could not shake off its pursuers. It dodged through streams and ditches, through the brackens and brambles. But still the black dog kept on its tail.

Very soon the hare grew tired, and the black dog managed to snap at its hind legs, drawing blood.

In a panic the hare changed direction and bolted straight into Ifan's grandmother's house.

When the huntsmen arrived they found Ifan's grandmother sitting in a chair, panting for breath, blood trickling from bite marks on her mud streaked legs.

Ifan never led the hunt again.

Ceridwen's Legacy

Whilst most accounts of mythological witches hold that they were wicked and performed many evil deeds, there is one story, that of Ceridwen, which is said to have left Wales with one of its greatest legacies.

Ceridwen was greatly annoyed that she had given birth to an ugly son. As the boy, whose name was Gwion, grew older he grew uglier. But Ceridwen, who was wise in the ways of dark magic, knew of no charms to cure his physical appearance.

She decided instead to create a charm to make him wise, and promised herself that if Gwion could not be handsome he could be clever. And if the charm didn't work, then she would kill him.

But preparation of the potion proved to be a long and arduous process. It had to be kept simmering and stirred constantly for exactly one year and a day. And during that time it had to be fed with rare herbs which Ceridwen could only find by walking for miles each day in search of them.

Gwion was given the task of stirring the potion during his mother's absence. All went well until the very last day of the process. Ceridwen was out hunting when Gwion accidently splashed a few drops on his hand. Instead of shaking them back into the cauldron Gwion licked them in order to taste his mother's magic.

It flowed through his body and he was immediately aware that this simple act had been enough to ruin the potion. But it had given him magical powers. Knowing his mother he was fully aware that she would kill him immediately upon her return.

Gwion decided to flee for his life, but Ceridwen pursued him relentlessly.

Gwion changed himself into a rabbit, but his mother changed into a fox. He changed into a fly. Ceridwen countered with the form of a swift.

Exhausted Gwion turned himself into a grain of wheat and hid in a large field. But his mother, whose powers of vision were great, transformed herself into a hen and ate the grain.

Reverting back to human form the witch discovered she was pregnant and nine months later gave birth to a son who could be none other than the very Gwion she had devoured.

This time the boy was formed with stunning beauty and she could tell he would be blessed with astounding wisdom. She decided not to kill him and instead cast the infant into the sea in a wickerwork basket.

The story would have ended there if Elphin, nephew of Maelgwn Gwynedd, had not been sailing by and heard the baby's cries.

He was rescued and renamed Taliesin who went on to become one of Wales' greatest bards and folk heroes, living, later in his life, on the banks of Llyn Geirionydd.

Taliesin had the powers of prophecy and science. He attended King Arthur's court where his stories foretold the coming of the Saxons, and of the oppression of Wales.

One of his surviving poems, said to date back to Arthurian times, translates thus:

> 'Their God they will praise,
> Their speech they will keep,
> Their land they will lose,
> Except wild Wales.'

And it must be said this prophecy did transpire.

Snakes & Dragons

In Welsh folklore snakes and dragons are related creatures. There existed a belief that the Viper, *Gwiber* in Welsh, could increase in size and grow wings if it drank the milk of a woman.

The *Brython* for 1861 states: 'If a snake chances to have the opportunity to drink a woman's milk it is certain to become a *gwiber*.' Of course, as previously mentioned, *gwiber* in modern usage refers to a viper. But the *Brython* explains that in folklore *Gwiber* actually means dragon or winged serpent.

Just how a snake managed to drink the milk of a woman is difficult to imagine. One theory, however, maintains that travelling women who were breastfeeding their babies often expressed unwanted milk onto the ground. Chance a snake upon this and we have a *Gwiber* (Dragon).

The Dragon of Denbigh

In the days when most of North Wales was woodland and the art of medicine was rudimentary, a large population of venomous snakes would probably have accounted for a relatively high number of deaths from snake bites.

It is not difficult to imagine, then, how the lowly snake became venerated to something as ferocious as a fire-breathing dragon. A person bitten might describe how the snake flew out of the undergrowth at him. Another might tell how the venom burned. To 'flew' in the retelling ascribe wings, and to 'burned' ascribe a breath of fire . . .

A dragon once terrorized the town of Denbigh, Clwyd. It had taken over the local ruined castle and was in the habit of darting out to attack and devour cattle, and even people.

The inhabitants of the town recruited the help of a local man called *Sion Bodiau* (Sir John of the Thumbs). This strange fellow had two thumbs on each hand. And so, in the estimation of the ordinary, five-fingered folk he surely possessed the power to rid them of the dragon.

Sir John was urged to approach the castle and tempt the dragon out. He had little choice as he rode towards it in full armour, lance held at the ready. Behind him was a population that would have murdered him had he refused. Ahead was a fire breathing dragon. Looking back at the women of the town, he decided to take his changes with the dragon.

This obliged with a grim rapidity, charging out of the castle and looming down on Sion Bodiau. But then the dragon halted short and stared down at the trembling man's hands, puzzling over the number of digits on display.

The grateful knight saw his opportunity and plunged his lance deep into the dragon's heart. He then drew his sword and chopped off its head.

Sion was a hero; the people ran through the town shouting 'Dim Bych, Dim Bych!' in celebration. And to this day even though the town is called Denbigh in English, that name is a corruption of the Welsh *'Dinbych'*, pronounced *'Dim-Bych'* locally ('no more dragon').

The Penhesgyn Prophecy

It was foretold by a prophet, who lived on the Isle of Anglesey, that a local heir to a fortune was soon to die from the bite of a huge viper or *Gwiber*.

The family who lived near Penhesgyn, had great respect for this particular prophet, so they sent their son to the mainland where he would be safe.

After his departure a trap was set for the *Gwiber*, and, a few days later, as the massive snake slithered towads the house it was attacked by a number of armed men who hacked the creature to death. Its body was buried nearby.

The young man was summoned home, but upon his arrival would not be appeased until he saw the creature that had intended to kill him.

He watched as workmen exhumed the remains, then seeing the ugly head for the first time he uttered an angry oath and aimed a hard kick at it.

But the Gwiber was still dangerous, even after death. Its forked tongue pierced the boy's leather sandal and penetrated his foot to the bone. Poison spread rapidly through his body and a few seconds later he collapsed.

Workmen carried the heir to a fortune into the house, where he died within an hour.

The Gwiber of Penmachno

There was a *Gwiber* in Penmachno that had lived there for hundreds of years. Not content with sprouting wings, or with being capable of turning into a dragon, this particular viper seems to have had its sights set on living forever.

An outlaw from Hiraethog decided it would be a feather in his cap if he could kill the ancient beast. But being a rather superstitious young man he first consulted a local wizard and asked what manner of death he could expect.

On his initial visit the reply was: 'From a viper's bite!' Highly dissatisfied, he visited the wizard a second time. 'You will die from a broken neck!' said the wise old man. The confused outlaw went there a third time and a grim faced magician warned: 'You will drown!'

The young man laughed. So much for wizards; no man could suffer three different deaths. Now he was certain he could approach the viper without fear.

He began to climb the rocks where it lived above a river. The young man grinned, sword at the ready. But then suddenly the *Gwiber* lashed out and bit him on the hand.

The outlaw fell from the rocks, breaking his neck, then rolled into the river where he drowned.

Thus all three prophecies were realised.

The Monster of Beaverpool

Attributed with exotic powers — the ability to make floods — the monster of *Llyn yr Afanc* (Beaver Pool) was causing great trouble for the people of the Vale of Conwy.

This mighty creature lived in a river pool not far from the town of Betws-y-coed. It was so large and strong nobody dared tackle it, and the citizenry faced a future littered with ruined crops and drowned cattle.

To their rescue came Hu Gadarn, the man who according to ancient writing first taught the *Cymry* (Welsh) to plough the land. He agreed to help, using his pair of mighty,long-horned oxen.

The only problem was how could he attach chains to the dratted creature? The pool was dark and deep and the Afanc was in his natural element. It would have been suicidal to have dived into the water in search of him.

They puzzled for many hours until a shrewd old peasant remarked that the Afanc was fond of pretty women and would probably come to the river bank if a suitable beauty was planted there as bait.

A brave young woman was duly found and the party proceeded to the pool. While the others hid themselves, the young woman sat on the bank and began to sing a lilting melody.

Sure enough it was not long before the dark waters rippled and a strange shape moved across the river. It paused for a few minutes, obviously observing the woman, who continued singing. Then slowly the Afanc emerged from the waters and crawled over to her.

With complete disregard for social niceties, the creature laid its ugly head in the girl's lap and rested one of its huge clawed hands on the softness of her breast.

Now the trap was sprung. Hu Gadarn and his local helpers dashed out and, before the Afanc could move, threw coils of chain around it. Bellowing with rage the monster leapt up, ripping off the poor young woman's breast, and plunged wildly back into the river.

But the chains held strong, and attached to the oxen, gradually, little by little, the Afanc was hauled out onto dry land.

Llyn yr Afanc

They could have killed it there and then, but Hu Gadarn was a saintly man with great respect for life. He decided to haul the creature to a place miles away where it would not be able to cause harm.

This proved a most difficult journey. So great was the strain at one point, one ox popped out its eye. It cried so much in the field where this happened that it formed a pool of tears. The field is now known as *Gwaun Llygad yr Ych* (Field of the Ox's Eye) and it is said that the pool, *Pwll Llygad yr Ych* (Pool of the Ox's Eye) never dries out — even though no spring or stream feeds it.

Eventually Hu Gadarn brought his charge to the banks of Llyn Glaslyn at the foot of Snowdon. He released the Afanc into the deep blue waters, where according to legend it still swims to this day.

Hu Gadarn is a particularly ancient Celtic hero. A sort of Welsh Noah, he is often depicted as possessing Godlike powers, and appears in many stories. There are also differing versions of the Afanc tale. It appears as far afield as in Hindu mythology, which credits the great god Vishnu with the destruction of a flood-bringing monster.

To say this indicates a Celtic link with the old Sanskrit speaking races of India and Afghanistan would be a gross conjecture. However, some historians favour a theory that the Celts were originally one of the Arian races of that region, who probably migrated across Europe as a roving band of mercenaries.

King Arthur in North Wales

Arthur, like Robin Hood, is a world famous hero whose deeds have been magnified by generations of people who dearly would have liked to believe that such a person existed. In fairness to them it is quite possible that the character is based on an actual person, probably a Celtic Prince, who once united his countrymen against the invading Saxons. And the Celts, as we have seen, are not the types to let a good story lie down and die of factuality.

Many parts of Britain claim Arthur Pendragon as their own. But most accounts indicate a link with either Cornwall — a Celtic region — or Wales. And the name *Pendragon* is an Anglo/Welsh name meaning Dragon's Head.

As far as North Wales is concerned, like many other regions, we claim Arthur fought his last battle here. The story goes something like this:

Arthur's army had left their fort at Dinas Emrys and were marching over a hill called Hafod y Borth to reach Tregalan at the upper end of Cwm Llan. It was during this march that they came face to face with an enemy force and a fierce battle commenced.

The Knights and Army of the Round Table fought well and drove the enemy up a pass towards Cwm Dyli. But as Arthur led his men to the top, a hail of arrows met him and the King fell mortally wounded. His Knights laid him down behind a rock where he died within minutes.

His body was covered over with stones to form a cairn, which is still there to this day and is called *Carnedd Arthur* (Arthur's Cairn). The mountain pass where he died is called *Bwlch y Saethau* (Pass of the Arrows).

After his tragic death, Arthur's surviving Knights ascended the ridge to a cave below the summit of Lliwedd. After the last warrior had entered, its entrance was sealed. This is known as *Ogof Llanciau Eryri* (Cave of the Young Men of Snowdon).

The Knights of the Round Table are said to be lying there still, their swords and armour at the ready, waiting for Arthur to rise from the dead. According to prophecy, he will do this on an occasion when Wales is in mortal danger.

The Shepherd and the Tomb

Many years later a shepherd was gathering his sheep on Lliwedd when one of his flock fell over a rocky cliff. He looked down and saw that the sheep had been saved by a narrow ledge.

Carefully the shepherd made his way down the slippery face and was surprised to see a faint light shining from the entrance to a cave.

He had heard many stories about Arthur's burial place, which was supposed to be packed with gold and jewels. Tempted by greed he pushed through the narrow opening and inside discovered hundreds of Knights in armour, lying as if asleep on the floor of the cave.

But the shepherd's eyes were fixed on a hoard of treasure beyond the warriors. Daringly he crept across the middle of the floor, intent upon stealing enough gold to last him a lifetime. But the unfortunate man had failed to notice a bell hanging from the ceiling. As he passed he brushed against it and a loud ringing echoed throughout the chamber.

The Knights awoke. Voices shouted, armour rattled, swords were lifted, and the shepherd — driven by panic — slipped back through the narrow entrance and scrambled to his home in the valley.

But if he thought he had escaped, he was mistaken. Over the next few weeks his health deteriorated and, mumbling something about the strange cave, he died — probably a victim of one of Merlin's curses, set to protect the cave.

Arthur and Rhitta Fawr

During happier times King Arthur built a reputation for himself as a slayer of giants, amongst other creatures. One day he was riding with a handful of Knights over the lower slopes of Aran Benllyn, south of Bala, when a huge giant stepped out into his path.

'I am Rhitta Fawr,' boomed the giant. 'Who would pass through my domain?'

Arthur identified himself as King of Britain. At this the giant mellowed and showed the King a strange cloak woven from oddly coloured materials.

'This,' explained Rhitta, 'is made from the beards of many kings.' The giant further explained that he would be deeply honoured to add Arthur's beard to the top of the cloak.

But the King had little patience with giants and refused to part with his facial hair. A highly insulted Rhitta then challenged Arthur to a duel and a fierce fight ensued.

The poor giant was no match for the agile and magical King and Rhitta soon lay dead on the ground. His body was buried at the summit of Aran Benllyn.

Other accounts place the event at the summit of Snowdon.

Prince Madog's Discovery of America

The discovery of America, as every schoolboy knows, is credited to the Genoese navigator Christopher Columbus in 1492. But many historians believe adventurers from other countries visited the New World long before that date. Some say Japanese fishermen, blown off course. Others say it was the Vikings.

But there is a possibility it was a Welshman who first discovered that mighty land.

During the 17th and 18th Centuries, as thousands of new settlers advanced Westwards across North America, a tribe of Indians, whose skin was much paler than usual, was discovered. Remarkably they spoke a language that was almost identical to Welsh.

But the story begins long before the days of pioneers and wagon trains. It begins in North Wales; land of Rumours and Oddities, witches, dragons. Land of brave princes:

Owain Gwynedd, ruler of the province in the 12th Century, had many sons and one of the youngest was a youth by the name of Madog, whose favourite pastime was sailing along the coast in his small boat.

Unlike others of his family, he preferred the open sea to the rocky wastes of Snowdonia. As a youth he made numerous friends amongst the fishermen and merchants who plied their trade along the coast, and learned many of the skills of seamanship from them.

Owain Gwynedd died in 1170. His decree divided the Kingdom between his two eldest sons, Dafydd and Hywel. But before long the pair had quarrelled and the threat of war loomed heavily over North Wales.

Madoc, now an adult, was approached by both sides but refused an alliance with either. He knew their only interest was in securing the fleet which he now effectively controlled.

Instead of involving himself and his friends in war, Madoc decided to fulfil a lifelong ambition — to sail westwards — where no man had gone before, beyond the furthest coast of Ireland, out into the mighty ocean where charts of the day said, 'here be dragons!'.

Madoc provisioned his new ship Gwennan Gorn and set sail from the mouth of the River Ganol, where Rhos-on-sea stands today.

After a rendezvous with his brother Rhiryd — who had lived in Ireland — the small fleet headed out into the Atlantic.

Nothing was seen of Madog for many years until, one day, the Gwennan Gorn reappeared over the horizon. Madog explained that he and his followers had found a great new land in the West, and appealed for volunteers to help settle there. After two or three months, many of the war-weary population decided to join, and so it was a large fleet that sailed for America for the last time.

Madog and his ships were never seen again.

The story might be difficult to swallow, but the people of Mobile Bay, Alabama, have erected a memorial which reads:

> *In memory of Prince Madoc, a Welsh explorer*
> *who landed on the shores of Mobile bay in 1170*
> *and left behind, with the Indians,*
> *the Welsh language.*

List of Map References and Nearby Places of Interest

Note: All map references given are approximate and are taken from the 1:50,000 Ordnance Survey Series.

The places of interest mentioned form a selection which is not exhaustive.

Llanfrothen O.S. 622413 Sheet No. 124
Port Meirion (2-3 miles) where T.V. Series 'The Prisoner' was filmed. Porthmadog, terminal of Ffestiniog narrow gauge railway.

Llangollen O.S. 053657 Sheet No. 117
Site of the International Eisteddfod, annually. Eliseg's Pillar. Valle Crucis Abbey. Llangollen Steam Railway. Chirk Castle. Riding Stables.

St Winifred's Well, Holywell O.S. 183763 Sheet No. 116
Military Museum. Basingwerk Abbey. Flint Castle.

Llangelynnin Old Church O.S. 752734 Sheet No. 115
for places of interest see Conwy.

MYSTERIOUS STONES

* Barclodiad y Gawres (Giantess's Apron) O.S. 716717 Sheet No. 115
Roman Road (Rowen to Aber).

Carreg Lleidr (Robber's Stone) O.S. 446843 Sheet No. 115
Wylfa Nuclear Power Station. Red Wharf Bay.

* Y Meini Hirion (The Tall Stones) O.S. 723747 Sheet No. 115
See the Stone Women of Moelfre.

Maetnwrog (St Twrog's Stone) O.S. 664405 Sheet No. 124
Rhaeadr Ddu (Black Waterfall) The Vale of Ffestiniog.

Maen y Bardd (The Poet's Stone) Burial Chamber O.S. 741718 Sheet No. 115
See Conwy

The Druids of Anglesey (See Anglesey generally)
See Carreg Lleidr

* The Stone Women of Moelfre O.S. 723747 Sheet No. 115
Memorial to Bachelor's Baby (Liberator Bomber).

* Red, White and Blue (Memorial as above) 716743 Sheet No. 115

The Curse of Nant Gwrtheyrn O.S. 350451 Sheet No. 123
Porthneigwl (Hell's Mouth Bay) for surfers. Plas-yn-rhiw, nr Aberdaron, 17th Century Manor House, overlooking the bay.

The Legend & Ghost of Beddgelert O.S. 591478 Sheet No. 115
Walks. The Aberglaslyn Pass.

The Dragons of Dinas Emrys O.S. 606492 Sheet No. 115
See Beddgelert above.

GHOSTS

The Golden Knight of Mold O.S. 244639 Sheet No. 117
Theatr Clwyd. Pony Trekking.

The Haunting of Plas Mawr (Conwy) O.S. 781776 Sheet No. 115
Conwy Castle and town walls. Telford's suspension Bridge. Aberconwy House. Nr. Conwy, Pinewood Stables, Pony Trekking.

The Ghostly Squire of Pentrefoelas O.S. 873515 Sheet No. 116
See Betws-y-coed.

The Mermaid's Curse, See Conwy above

SUNKEN CITIES

Llys Helig (Map reference not available, location unknown)

Llyn Tegid (Lake Bala) O.S. 920351 Sheet No. 125
Cyffdy Farm Park. National White Water Centre, Canoeing. Bala Water Sports Centre.

LAKE LEGENDS

Dark Water, Red Altar (Llun Dulyn) O.S. 702665 Sheet No. 115
* Easy Access to the Carneddau Ridge.

Llyn Morwynion (Lake of the Maidens) O.S. 738423 Sheet No. 124
See Ffestiniog. (Huw Llwyd)

The Floating Island of Llyn Dywarchen O.S. 561543 Sheet No. 115
See Beddgelert. Starting Point for Snowdon Ranger walk to the summit of Snowdon, Rhyd Ddu, Youth Hostel.

Llyn Idwal (Idwal's Lake) O.S. 645595 Sheet No. 115
Rock climbing country. A5 to Bethesda, Bangor & Penrhyn Castle.

DEVILS, WITCHES & CONJURORS

The Devil's Tree O.S. 794800 Sheet No. 115
Llanrhos Church. Llandudno (well known tourist resort with many amenities).

The Witches of Betws-y-coed O.S. 794465 Sheet No. 115
Swallow Falls, Fairy Glen. Capel Garmon Burial Chamber. Gwydir Castle (Llanrwst). See the Monster of Beaverpool.

Huw Llwyd's Pulpit O.S. 705412 Sheet No. 124
Tomen-y-Mur, (Roman Fort); Maentwrog. Trawsfynydd Nuclear Power Station. Tan-y-Grisiau Hydro Electric Power Station and Stwlan Dam. Llechwedd Slate Quarry.

SNAKES AND DRAGONS

The Dragon of Denbigh O.S. 050660 Sheet No. 116
Denbigh Castle and Town Walls. Denbigh Friary. St Hilary's Chapel. The Vale of Clwyd.

The Penhesgyn Prophecy O.S. 534371 Sheet No. 115
Numerous ancient monuments in vicinity. Also see Carreg Lleidr.

The Gwiber of Penmachno O.S. 770524 Sheet No. 115
Tŷ Mawr. Dolwyddelan Castle.

KING ARTHUR IN NORTH WALES

* The Shepherd & The Tomb O.S. 623533 Sheet No. 115 (Summit of Lliwedd)

Snowdon Railway. Llanberis. Numerous walks.

Arthur & Rhitta Fawr O.S. 867243 Sheet No. 125 (Arran Benllyn)

See Llyn Tegid (Lake Bala) under Sunken Cities.

Prince Madog's Discovery of America O.S. 829815 Sheet No. 116 (Rhos-on-sea)

Colwyn Bay. St Trillo's Church. Eirias Park and Leisure Centre.

* For properly equipped hillwalkers only

Folklore

Supernatural Clwyd
The Folk Tales of North-East Wales 210pp. £4.50. 0-86381-127-2
Many illustrations and photographs.
Now, for the first time the supernatural folk tales of Clwyd
have been collected together. Many have not seen print for
over a hundred years.
Richard Holland

Haunted Clwyd 144pp. £3.50. 0-86381-218-X. *Many illustrations.*
From Clwyd's rich heritage of folklore to present day first
hand accounts, here are phantoms of all description, homely
or terrifying.
Richard Holland

Bye-gones 120pp. £3.50. 0-86381-239-2.
Old folklore collected by Richard Holland; black & white illustrations.
Old volumes of *Bye-Gones*, a periodical published between
1871 and 1939, are a treasure trove of anecdotes relating to
Wales and the Border Counties.
Richard Holland

Welsh Witches and Warlocks 120pp. £2.25. 0-86381-068-3.
Wales has always been known as the land of the strange or
legends of mystery and superstition, going back to its Celtic
origin. In this book there is a collection of forty traditional
tales about Welsh witches and wizards.
Jane Pugh

GWASG CARREG GWALCH
12 Iard yr Orsaf, Llanrwst, Gwynedd, Wales LL26 0EH
Tel: 01492 642031   Fax: 01492 641502